Simply Science

ELECTRIC ENERGY

Felicia Law

Illustrations: Steve Boulter & Xact Studio

Diagrams: Karen Radford

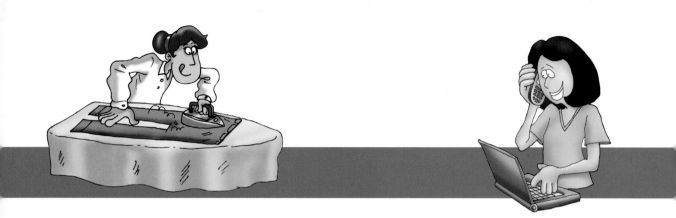

AUTHOR: FELICIA LAW
CONSULTANT: STEVE WAY
ILLUSTRATORS:

STEVE BOULTER
XACT STUDIO

DESIGN: RALPH PITCHFORD

ISBN 978-1-906292-11-9
Printed in China

PHOTO CREDITS:

p.4-5 Iksung Nah/Alamy.
p.6 Andre Seale/Alamy.
p.7 Jhaz Photography/Shutterstock Inc.
p.8 Eugene Comstock/Shutterstock Inc.
p.9 Art Directors.
p.10 Pchemyan Georgiy/Shutterstock Inc.
p.11 (tl) Walter Matheson/Shutterstock Inc.,
(tr) Thomas Mounsey/Shutterstock Inc.
p.12 PHOTOTAKE Inc./Alamy.
p.13 Jeremy Walker/SCIENCE PHOTO LIBRARY
p.14 (b) N.A., Switzerland/Shutterstock Inc.
p.14-15 Vario Images GmbH & Co.KG/Alamy.
p.16 Peter Bowater/Alamy.
p.17 Lester Lefkowitz/CORBIS.
p.18 (bc) Michele Otri/Shutterstock Inc.,
(r) Kondrachov Vladimir/Shutterstock Inc.
p.21 Harald Høiland Tjøstheim/Shutterstock Inc.
p.22 Tomasz Trojanowski/Shutterstock Inc.
p.23 (tl) David Andrew Gilder/Shutterstock Inc.,
(cr) Yanta/Shutterstock Inc.,
(bl) Feng Yu/Shutterstock Inc.,
(br) 4uphoto.pt/Shutterstock Inc.
p.25 Polina Lobanova/Shutterstock Inc.
p.28 (tr) Chinch Gryniewicz/CORBIS,
(cr) William Casey/Shutterstock Inc.
p.29 (t) Robert Francis/CORBIS,
(br) Debra Weatherley.

Cover
Jhaz Photography/Shutterstock Inc.

Simply Science

ELECTRIC ENERGY

Contents

What is electricity?

You may think that electricity is just what makes lights come on or heats the iron up. You know it runs round your house in wires and is there when you flick a switch on the wall. But electricity everywhere! It's in the air and the ground, in every object around – and it's even in YOU!

Electricity is everywhere and it helps:

light things up ...

heat things up ...

send messages ...

power vehicles ...

make machines work.

Electricity all around

If you've ever seen a thunderstorm, you'll probably have seen a flash of lightning streak across the sky. Lightning is a great spark of electricity in the air.

Your body is full of electricity too, although it's nowhere as powerful as that lightning bolt! Your heart makes tiny amounts of electricity and these help it to beat properly. Your brain uses electricity too, to send messages all over your body through nerves.

Electric eels

Electric eels produce electricity in their bodies – just like all animals. But the electric eel uses it as a weapon. This fish is found in the Amazon and Orinoco rivers in South America. It uses its electric power to stun its prey and also to shock its enemies and drive them away. In fact, it can produce enough electricity in its body to light 12 light bulbs!

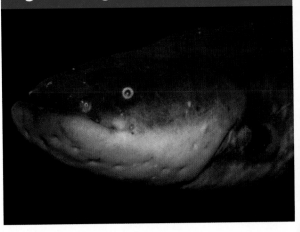

Lightning

Lightning is a powerful electric spark. A single spark is so strong that it can burn the ground or even set trees and houses on fire. It can also kill a person with the force of its shock.

A lightning conductor is a thick wire. Its job is to carry lightning away and prevent damage to a building. One end is fixed to the top of a building. The other is buried in the ground.

Moving electrons

Everything around you has some electricity in it. It contains tiny, invisible particles of electricity called electrons.

The electrons don't normally flow as electricity, they just zip around and around where they are. But in some kinds of materials, the electrons can be pushed along, moving other electrons with them and creating a stream of electrons. It is this moving stream that is an electric current.

atom   electron

Each electron only has a small amount of energy. It only moves a short distance when pushed. But inside a wire or battery, there are millions and millions of electrons. So when you turn on a switch, you start a big stream of electrons moving.

Conductors

Electrons move easily through some kinds of materials - these are known as conductors. One of the best conductors is the metal, copper. This is why many of the electric wires used in your house are made from copper.

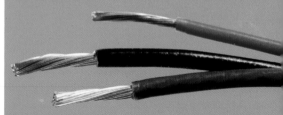

Insulators

Electrons can't flow at all through other materials - we call these insulators. Plastic is a good insulator. It stops the current flowing where it might be dangerous. Copper wires are covered in plastic so they can't harm you.

Electrons

An electron is a tiny speck of matter. It is one of the parts of an atom. Everything in the world is made of atoms and all atoms have one or more electrons spinning around their centre, called the nucleus.

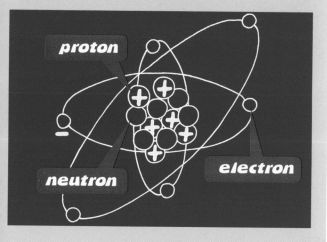

There are three parts to an atom.
The neutrons are at the centre.
They give off no charge.

The protons are also in the centre, or nucleus, of the atom.
They have a positive charge.

The electrons zip around the nucleus in wide orbits.
They have a negative charge.

Static electricity

You can see electricity at work in static electricity. This is a kind of energy that builds up when electrons move from one object to another. One object gets the electrons, the other loses them. If you use a plastic comb on a dry day you can feel static electricity in your hair; it may even crackle. You can sometimes feel a tiny shock when you touch something metal, like a door knob.

9

Mr Volt and Mr Amp

You can make a bulb light up by using two wires to join it to a battery. The battery pushes electrons around the wires and through the bulb, making it glow. The strength of this push is measured in volts. The more volts a battery has, the stronger the push.

V is for volt!
The volt, or V for short, is a unit of measurement. Voltage is measured with a voltmeter. The volts supplied to a house are between 110 and 230 volts.

The word volt comes from the name of the man who invented the first battery - an Italian called Alessandro Volta. His battery made a form of energy. This happened when the metals copper and zinc were put in salt water. The salt water began to react on the metals causing electrical energy to be given off.

Batteries
Modern batteries are made up of layers of chemicals inside a metal can. When the battery starts working, some of the chemicals break away and start eating at the metal container. The change to the can creates an electric current that flows out of the battery.

A is for amp!

The ampere, or A for short, is the unit for measuring an electric current. Amperes are often called amps. A current of about half an amp lights up an ordinary electric light bulb. 1 amp = about 6 million, million, million electrons flowing every second!

An ammeter is the instrument used to measure the strength of an electric current in amperes.

The word amp comes from the name of the French scientist who invented a way of measuring an electric current, André-Marie Ampère.

Ampère was a brilliant mathematician. Together with other scientists, he showed how an electric current automatically produced a magnetic field.

More importantly, he helped show how a powerful magnetic force can be created by electricity. This force is called 'electromagnetism'.

11

Electromagnetism

An electromagnet is made with a special coil of wire wound around an iron rod. The rod works like a magnet when an electric current is switched on and flows through the wire. When the current is switched off, the electromagnet loses its magnetism.

How a magnet works

A magnet can be made from a bar of material, like iron, which attracts other objects containing iron. Magnets are surrounded by a pulling force known as a magnetic field. The field helps the magnet pull other metals towards it and push them away.

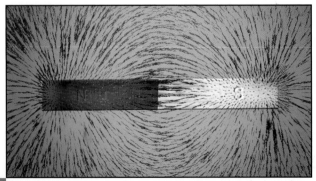

Generator

If a magnet is spun around in a coil of wire its magnetic field causes an electrical current to flow in the wires. A big magnet in a big coil generates a very powerful flow of electricity. This is how electricity is generated in power stations.

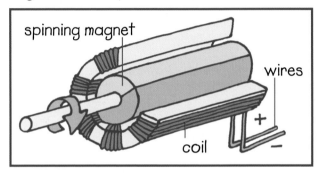

spinning magnet

wires

coil

+

−

Electric motor

if an electric current is already flowing in the coil, then it will cause the magnet to spin because its poles are attracted to the electrical charge in the wires. The rod, which is attached to the magnet, also spins and can be used to turn a wheel or a fan! This arrangement is called an electric motor.

How electromagnets work

Huge electromagnets are used in scrapyards to help lift and move great chunks of metal from place to place.

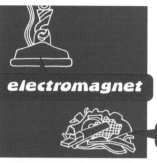

electromagnet

scrap metal

1. The electromagnet hangs from the hook of a large crane. It is lowered towards the chunk of scrap metal.

2. The electric current is switched on and the electromagnet acts like a strong magnet, attracting the scrap metal.

3. The crane lifts its load of scrap and moves it to another place.

4. The electric current is switched off. The magnet loses its power to attract and the scrap drops to the ground.

Moved by electricity

Electric motors can be used to power all sorts of machines. Electricity can be supplied to an electric motor by a battery or by connecting it to an electricity supply.

Vehicles such as trains, trams and dodgem cars need to be able to move without being fixed to the electrical circuit. They use an aerial to rub against the wires and power them along.

The pantograph, or aerial, on the roof of this tram rubs against the overhead wires.

Moving currents

An alternating current (AC) is an electric current that behaves in a special way. The current grows stronger then weaker and then changes direction. This happens over and over again many times each second. This is the type of current produced by generators, so it's the type of current that's supplied to your home.

A direct current (DC) is another kind of electric current. It flows steadily through wires in one direction only. This kind of current flows from batteries.

15

At the power station

Most of the electricity we use in our homes is made in huge power stations.

Inside the power station, great wheels called turbines are turned by the force of hot steam. The wheels are made with curved blades and as they spin, they turn a pole attached to a generator. The generator makes electrical energy and the transformer changes the electricity to the correct voltage to send to users.

Super-hot steam hits the blades of this turbine, making it spin.

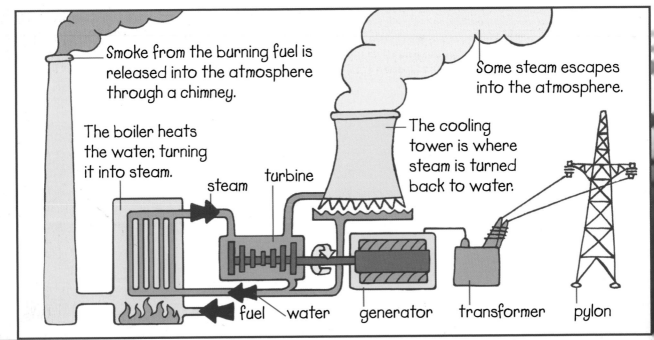

Smoke from the burning fuel is released into the atmosphere through a chimney.

The boiler heats the water, turning it into steam.

Some steam escapes into the atmosphere.

The cooling tower is where steam is turned back to water.

steam

turbine

fuel   water   generator   transformer   pylon

Hydro-electric power

Some power stations don't use steam to turn the turbines. They use fast-flowing water as it drops through pipes from the top of a reservoir. The water pushes the turbine blades as it rushes past, making electricity.

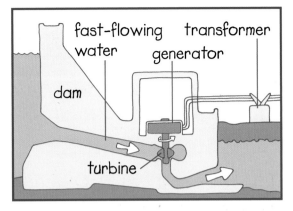

fast-flowing water

transformer

generator

dam

turbine

Dams can be huge! This is the Hoover Dam, in the USA, which is 221m high and 379m wide! The dam forms Lake Mead, one of the biggest man-made lakes in the world.

Once the electricity has been generated at the power station, it must be carried to your home. It is brought there through a system of underground and overground cables. This system is known as a grid.

Electricity is carried from power stations where it is generated to towns and cities. It is sometimes carried across the countryside along huge overhead cables held up by towers known as pylons.

A pylon is a kind of tower which is made from steel or wood. The cables hang from glass insulators fixed to the pylons. The insulators stop the current escaping down the pole and hurting anyone.

Electricity supply grid

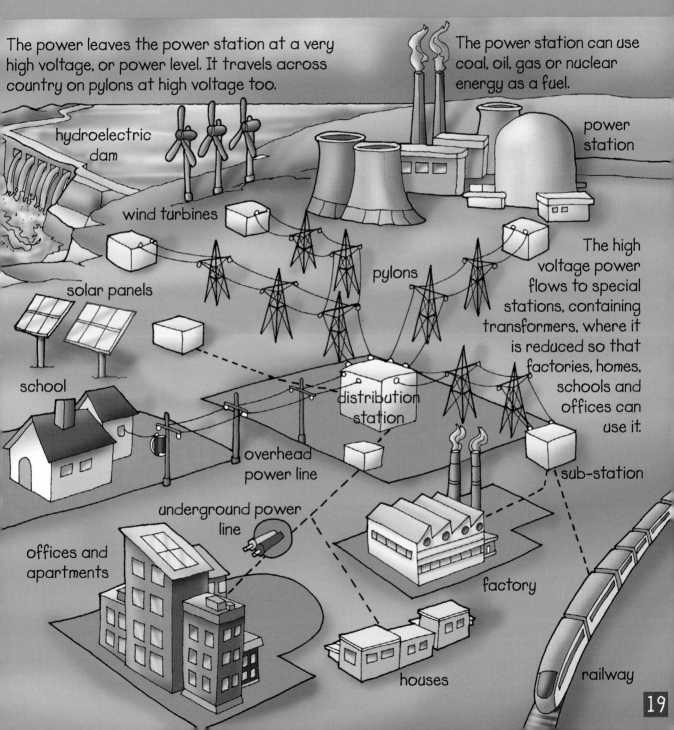

The power leaves the power station at a very high voltage, or power level. It travels across country on pylons at high voltage too.

The power station can use coal, oil, gas or nuclear energy as a fuel.

The high voltage power flows to special stations, containing transformers, where it is reduced so that factories, homes, schools and offices can use it.

hydroelectric dam

wind turbines

power station

solar panels

pylons

school

distribution station

overhead power line

sub-station

offices and apartments

underground power line

factory

houses

railway

Making it safe

Electricity may be useful, but it can be dangerous, particularly because it's invisible. When it reaches your home, it enters on the mains supply cable.

From here wiring circuits in the walls, floors and ceilings connect to all the light switches and electric plugs around the home. You can safely use these to help light up a room, turn on the television or heat the oven.

When electricians installed the wiring in your home, they used special connections and circuits to make sure the electricity is safe to use.

BEWARE, SHORT CIRCUIT!

If the plastic covering that protects electric wires wears through, it may allow the two wires to touch. The electric current will then be able to flow from one wire into the other. This is called a short circuit and it's dangerous! The wires will overheat or spark, which might cause a fire.

NEVER throw water on a fire caused by an electrical fault. Water conducts electricity!

WARNING

Mains electricity is dangerous! NEVER PLAY with electric sockets or wires or touch them with wet hands. An electric shock could kill you!

Switching off the current

Fuse

A fuse is a thin piece of wire. It is part of an electric circuit. If there is too much current, the fuse becomes hot and melts. This safely switches off the electricity.

Circuit breaker

A circuit breaker is a kind of electric switch. It is connected to an electric circuit and switches off the electric current if too much suddenly flows through the circuit.

Earth wire

An earth wire is found inside most electric cables. It is part of the electricity supply of a house. It is also found in the cables that lead from any electric appliance. If there is a fault, the earth wire leads the electric current safely away.

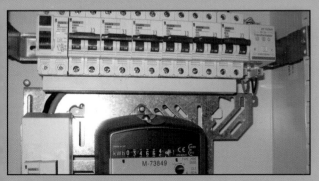

A fuse box above an electricity meter. Different areas of the house are kept safe by different fuses.

A switch is a way of turning an electric current on ...

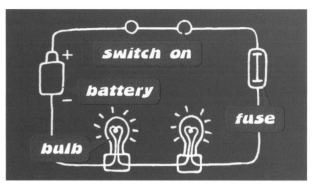

...or off.

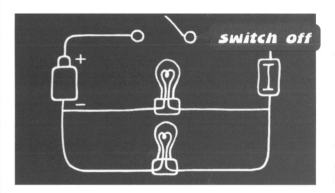

Inside the wire

Most of the cable you see in your home holds 3 wires. One is usually a brown wire that carries the current from the fusebox. This is called the live wire. The blue wire carries the power back to the fusebox to make the circuit. The green and yellow stripy wire is the earth wire.

Heating up

As electrons push through a thin wire, they give off energy in the form of heat. This is because they're all bumping into each other and the atoms in the wire. The wire gives off heat, which we can use in different ways.

Electrical fires, irons, kettles, toasters, hairdryers – all heat up in the same way. An electric current passes along thin wire once you switch them on. The wire is made of a special material, usually tungsten, that conducts the current easily, and heats up as it does.

toaster

hairdryer

kettle

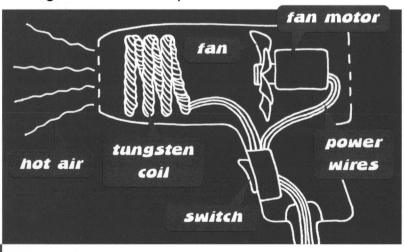

fan motor

fan

hot air

tungsten coil

power wires

switch

Heating appliances

washing machine

iron

cooking ring

A Kilowatt

A kilowatt is a unit of measurement that measures the power given off by an electric gadget. One kilowatt is 1000 watts.

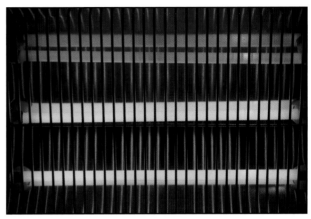

This electric fire has a power of 3 kilowatts.

Tungsten

Tungsten is very hard metal. It is used in the heating coils inside many electrical gadgets, especially those that heat up to a high temperature. Tungsten has the highest melting point – a massive 3,410 degrees Centigrade – and the highest strength at temperatures above 1650 °C of all metals. When steel is mixed with tungsten, it becomes even tougher!

Switching on the light

Thomas Alva Edison, an American inventor, grew up in a world where homes were lit by gas lamps, and sometimes - candles. You couldn't light up a house with the flick of a switch - not in those days!

A bright idea

1. Thomas Edison was a bright young man who had just arrived in the city of New York. He had many ideas in his brain - inventions that would change people's lives.

2. As the result of an infection, Edison was deaf. He invented devices to help deaf people. He also improved machines that sent telegraphs. In fact, he thought up over 1,000 inventions in his lifetime.

Low-energy light bulbs

Modern low-energy light bulbs use only about $\frac{1}{5}$ the power of standard light bulbs but can last around 15 times longer, so they save a lot of energy. The bulbs are coated on the inside with a chemical called phosphor. A burst of energy when they're switched on excites gas inside them, and makes the phosphor glow.

3. But he is best known for inventing the first commercial light bulb. He developed a glass bulb that wouldn't melt from the heat of a glowing electric wire inside. The secret was to take out all the air trapped in the glass, creating what is known as vacuum.

4. The electric current was passed through a tiny string of carbon which made it glow. A switch could stop and start the current flow.

Gadget power

You probably couldn't live without electricity. Modern homes depend on it for lighting, heating, cooking and washing – and to power all those useful gadgets, especially the ones that bring you entertainment.

Easy swaps!

Electric tin opener
Use a hand one and some muscle power.

Iron
Wear clothes that don't crease or spread them under your mattress at night.

Hairdryer
Shake and towel dry your hair instead. It's far better for it anyway!

Power cut!

Oh dear! The electricity supply is cut and there's no more power coming to your home. What will you do? It's time to remember how people managed before the days of electric power!

There's no heating so it's time to chop some wood and light a fire. Or there are heaters that burn oil and give out a fierce heat.

Food rotting in the refrigerator? Time to think about buying fresh food and cooking it on the day.

The lights have gone out. It's time to find some candles. But take care of the flames.

Bring out the batteries

Although your power supply is off, you can still use all the gadgets that will run on stored electricity - on batteries.

Time to put on an extra woolly and long socks.

The electric clocks have stopped. Time to wind up the clockwork one, But remember, it will need resetting as the spring inside winds down. And with no alarm, you'll have to rely on the Sun, like your ancient ancestors!

No television! What did your grandparents do when they were children? Read books, put on puppet plays, play games round the house, generally have a great time!

Computer down! Homework must go manual - time to get out reference books and use the library.

Electricity in the future

We take electricity for granted but only a few hundred years ago, people had to live without it. And they did fine – mostly! They burned wood for fuel and heat and to cook their food. They used the power of wind and water to drive their machines, and lit wax candles to light their homes.

Today, scientists are warning us that we must return to these old ways. Not only are our fuel suppllies about to run out, but they are doing a great deal of damage to our planet.

Solar power

Some solar panels can be used for changing sunlight energy to electricity. They are really useful in remote places – and on orbiting satellites!

Wind power

Most modern wind power is generated on wind farms. tall poles hold turbine blades that are turned by the force of the wind. Large scale wind farms provide power for national electrical grids while smaller individual turbines can provide electricity to an isolated building.

This is a geothermal power station at Wairakei, New Zealand. It produces over 4% of the country's electricity!

Clockwork power!

This "clockwork" radio has a small generator inside it – when it's "wound up" it produces enough electricity to power the radio for about 30 minutes!

Geothermal power

This kind of power comes from energy trapped in the Earth's rocks. This often rushes to the surface in the form of steam. The force of the steam can be used to drive turbines and make electricity. Hot water below the ground can also be pumped to the surface and piped to homes to be used for heating.

Electricity Quiz

1. What are the tiny parts of atoms that carry electricity?

_____

2. Who invented the world's first battery?

_____

3. What feature of electricity is measured in Amps or Amperes?

_____

4. What happens to an electromagnet when you switch it on?

_____

5. Which parts of your body use electricity to send messages?

_____

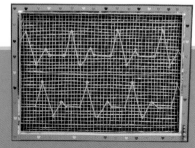

6. What part of a power station makes the magnets in the generator spin?

_____

7. What type of electricity can be made at a dam?

_____

8. What happens when a fuse wire melts?

_____

9. Which special metal has a melting point of 3410 degrees C?

_____

10. What important electrical device did Thomas Alva Edison develop?

Index